Poems for explosion

JOHN G. HALL

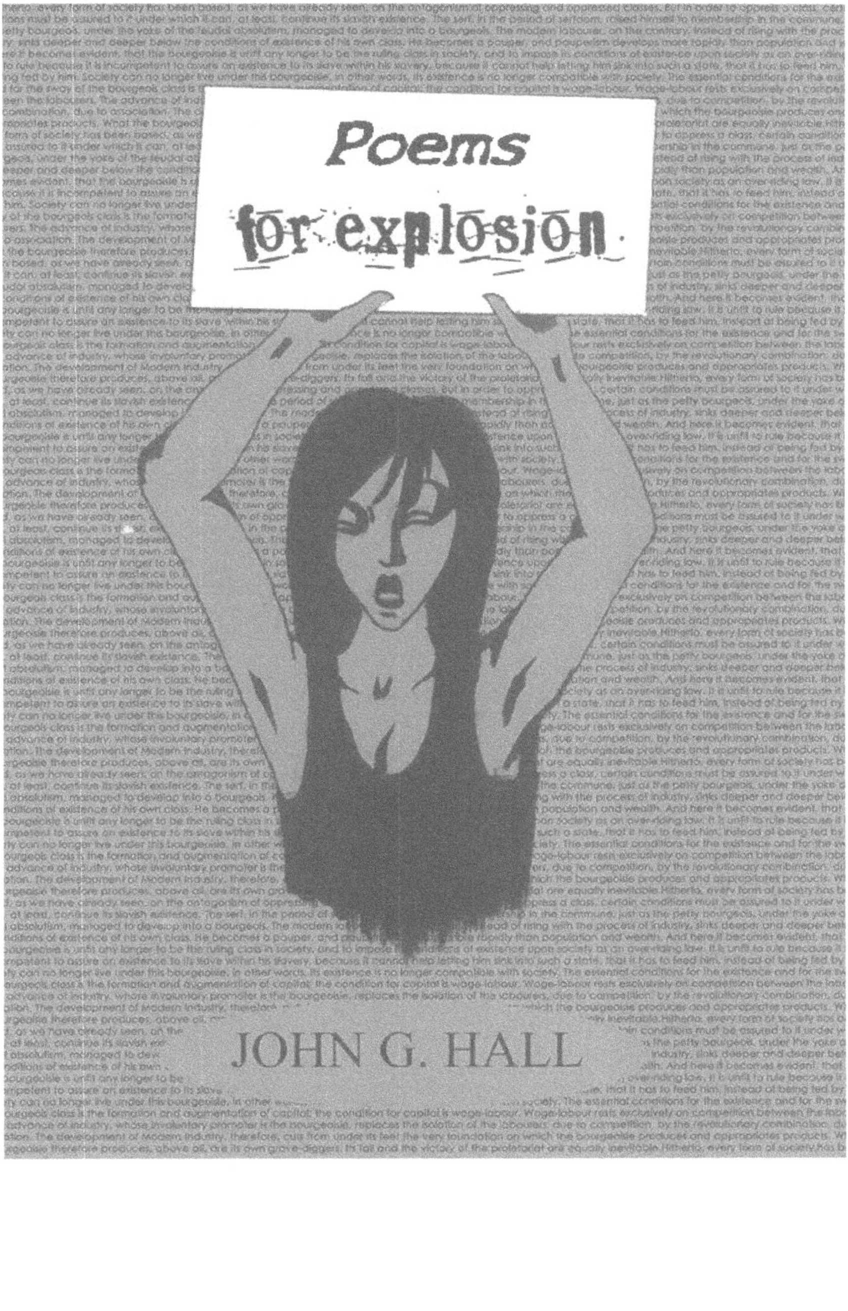

Poems for Explosion
Published as CC#58
ISBN 978-1-940996-14-1

Poems © 2015 by John G. Hall
Illustrations © 2015 by Becky Mackay
Foreword © 2015 by Sue Fox
Cover image © 2015 by Charlotte Henson

No part of this book may be reproduced in any manner whatsoever without written permission except in the case of brief quotations embodied in critical essays and articles.

1st printing, 26 February 2015

Crisis Chronicles Press
John Burroughs, editor
3344 West 105th Street #4
Cleveland, Ohio 44111
crisischronicles.com
ccpress.blogspot.com
facebook.com/crisischroniclespress

Foreword

John G. Hall is a playful punk-rock poet, with "kick arse" words that resonate like playground rituals. John is irreverent and feisty, guttural and provocative, brutally honest and downright rude.

He will pluck your eyes out without mercy and deliver you at the gate like a slaughtered sacrifice. He will make you weep into your core with an unpredictable savagery of tender words. John's poems are reflections upon love, memory and death, the unseen and the unborn.

They are like stainless steel balls in a pinball machine, impossible to destroy or forget, like tiny atom bombs that go off in your heart.

He evokes the bitter-sweet, the rhapsody of infatuated love and obsession, shows the disdain of rejection and lies. He draws the scar. He offers you the devil.

The trail of time touches and disintegrates everything in its path, just like the fleeting moment of a bubble.

John has an apocalyptic voice, bohemian too and "in your fucking face."

He makes you surrender to your unconsciousness until you are left with your own screaming silent truth.

—Sue Fox, lecturer in Film & Media Studies at the Manchester School of Art, Manchester Metropolitan University

Dedicated to John Thomas Hall
Love's labourer lost 17th January 2014
xx

Thank you Mr. Cameron for teaching our children about the need for revolution

fifty thousand tuning forks vibrating tongues

feeling the fascist penetration of their hearts

trembling, chanting, laughing, dreaming, daring,

they reach a sweet spot, a perfect pitched note

that harmonizes the capitalist discordant screech

of claws pawing at their young divining imaginations

forget 1984 it's the Dickens that's going on some more

a ripping off of warmth and pity in favor of mental chains

of genetic judgment and lies dipped in prejudiced hatreds

but here on the tarmac sounding board of a generation

the inner ears of young conscience recognize the drum

of money's inhuman war undeclared upon powerless poor

of wealth's fascist scheme to tie up their dreams in fears

this bile faced government is an untrustworthy uncle busy

fiddling with your children while you do not believe your eyes

and punish the victims for their weeping selfish suffering sighs

you built a safe place, a soft touch, a society that gave a care,

this bile faced government is busy fiddling with it, raping its easy

ways, beating its weak arms, burning its thin skin, torturing its

dreams with anxious nightmares and threats of stone veined laws

but now the rising imagination has caught the scent of this rich abuse and is breaking free in the streets and is coming your monster's way

with perfect pitched forks and deep throated torch and short fused cause

the wind moves the top of the trees first but soon the storm will uproot

your molesting malevolence and castrate your cock and bull system's balls

thank you Mr. Cameron for teaching our children about the need for revolution.

Kill the Mickey Mouse that lives in your head, it wants your brain for cheese

It wants to dandify death, it wants to kiss better Armageddon, it wants to lie down with your Lion and turn him into lamb, it wants to dandify genocide, it wants to loop a laugh in your soul that will drown out the screams of bombs it wants to lead rich rats to your heart, it whistles while they work at numbing your righteous nerves, it calls for laughter and pratfalls to be your manifestos, it fancies dressing you up in red noses and nurses' uniforms, while it bathes in lemonade champagne and smokes ginger bread cigars, it dances on each human right's grave, 'cheer up it may never happen' it squeals, while it happens to your family again and again, 'you've got to laugh' it whispers this, insists on it, it wraps up horror, rape, war, murder, corruption, violence, betrayal, poverty, debt and death, relax, your head can take it, it only exists between your ears, what are the moaning commies going on about, they just need a good fucking Xbox, or a good fucking iPod, or a good fucking night out, or a good fucking fucking, whether they want it or not, aaaah get over it punk, it says all this with a child light voice to conjure up your innocence, it counts on it, it arms your children with dreams of slippery coins to lead them better to oblivion, this human farce is too serious to be left to comics and rodents, today it sits on Clegg and Cameron's lap blowing them each time they cut another vein, it laps up your youth, with its black inky lips, gobbles on your love, sucks out your hopes, then sings a song of Hollywood gossip and the three zillion to one chance you could make it to the top, it wants you sitting comfortably while it begins gnawing at your world, while it gnaws at your hard won prizes, while it gnaws on you. Yeah! Kill the Mickey Mouse that lives in your head, it wants your brains for cheese. Kill that fucking Mickey Mouse because it will fuck you!

Bully for you

the bully for you is the bully of me

the good news you bring reads devilish

the lucky breaks cursed and crippling,

the win lies on the surface of the big lose

the beautiful skin holds the fascist muscle

win, win, win, win, win, win, win, win, win, WIN

the arms jerk into their favorite winning salute,

it's a zig-hail happy slap, round up the lazy losers

force feed them forced labors, gang and chain

them into non-existence, into characters for horror

comics and children's bedtime story books about

ruling class princesses and working class ogres

because you see the bully for you is the bully of me,

if this baleful diatribe sounds bitter so much the better

if this dirge depresses you well I'm sorry about that never

for this view from the bottom of the pile is justice finally arrived

the bullied having the bus fare to bully you back to the cold side of town.

The poor should be unheard and unseen (unless it's good T.V.)

the poor should

have the grace

to look poor, be

dirty, be bruised,

be dim, be vicious,

be sinners, be thin,

be dressed in rags,

be small, be bony,

be slow, be sad, be

silent, be mad, be bad,

be glad for everything

thrown their weird way,

be on their knees, be

on all fours, be animals,

be prisoners of their own

dreams, be dead quickly,

be organ donors, be cheaply

made warriors, be unquestioning,

be consumers, be recycled, be

guilty bleeders, be murderers, be

child killers, be incest T.V. stars, be

circus clowns, be subjects for docu-
soaps, be charity cases, be drunks,
be junkies, be tramps, be artless, be
heartless, be strangers, be bad sons, be
bad daughters, be grateful, be quiet, be
ogres, be whores, be loveless, be
rutting machines, be thugs, be proudly
soundly beaten, be jailed, be starved, be
patronized, be poisoned, be suicided, be
driven insane, be street characters, be
workshop exercises, be passengers, be
pedestrians, be unheard and unseen, be
sick, be disease ridden, be fuck ups, be
down beats, be sliced up in the name
of science, be road kill, be dumb bastards,
be the shit on the rich man's shoe, be rain
running in the gutters, be broken bottles, be
a waste of time, be unproductive, be unprofitable,
be burning skin going up a chimney, be wired up
to the mains by brave soldiers, be fed endless
gadgets and chemical oblivions, be cut off from
community, be isolated, be polluted, be dimmed

down, be lied to by truth tellers, be defeated, be

left naked and bloody, be the subject of poor laws, be

the crown's property, be lost in the dark provoked

prejudices of the slaved masses, be spat on, be

burned out, be whipped, be sterilized, become a disturbing list

of torture and terror and injustice that interrupts your pleasant night out,

your important relaxation, better be human kind before it's too late my friends

because someone somewhere is placing your name on their bloody 'B' list.

Oh Yeah, then they will decide what you should be

and then to be or not to be will not be the question

it will be the powers that be that answer for thee.

Be refugee, be homeless, be claimant, be student,

be single parent, be elderly, be militant feminist, be

terrorist, be deviant, be trade unionist, be socialist, be

benefit cheat, be ugly, be fat, be small, be old, be crippled, be

crazy, be Jew, be Palestinian, be black, be poor, be someone

they can kick around some more, be blamed for the crashing world

of war and corruption, may be it is YOU and NOT the yellow brick bankers,

may be it is YOU and NOT the monkey winged war machine mongers that

have responsibility for it all after all, after all the honest to goodness alibis.

To be or not to be is still the question, still the Canary singing in the mind.

To be or not to be is still the answer, still the Canary singing in the mind.

To be is to be my answer and this warning shall be my birdsong

your answers and your songs are for you to find, for you to sing.

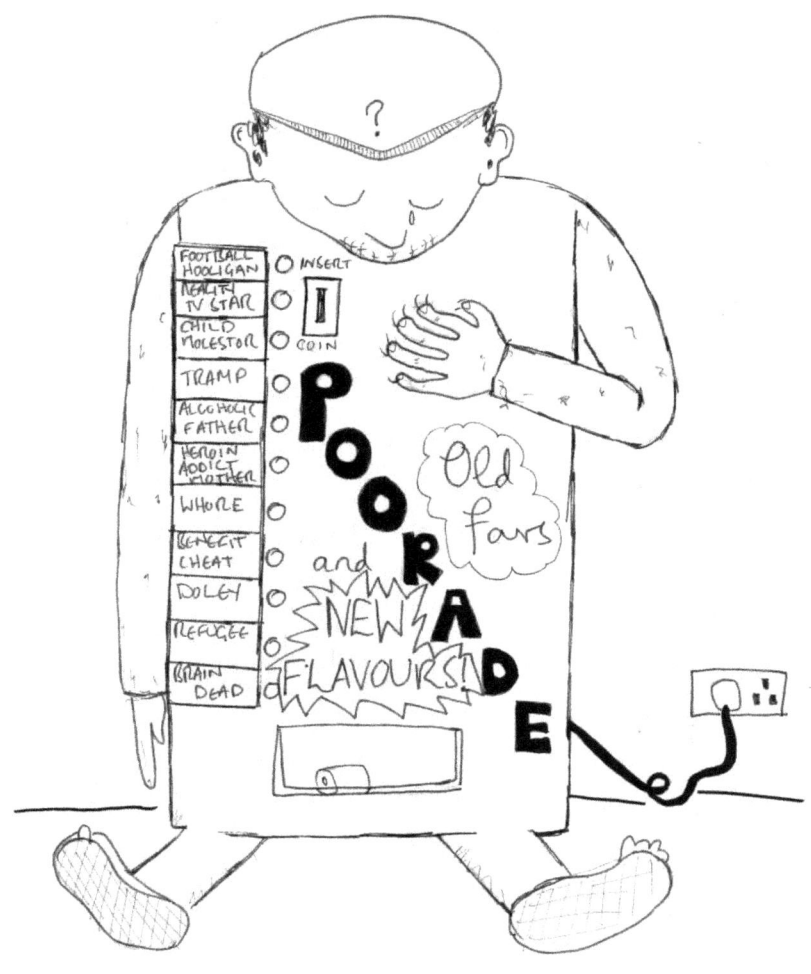

BP Black Mass

An ocean of tongues

lap at the waves of bull's blood

all blind eyes see the same night.

A smashed earthen heart

lies bleeding ancient sunlight

into greed's fire damaged sea.

Pilate washed hands in water

money anoints itself with oils

while nature hangs on nails.

Forgive them not father

for they know what they

did do and will continue.

Our kingdom will come

on the sea as it does

in wars and famines.

Amen O when

O when Amen.

Gunshawe *

I.

Black car flash black Glock 17

the estate recoils from the streets

bolted doors are bolted more

family feud is always rumored

I Google Glock 17 come up with

laser blue toy replicas and blanks,

better avoid walking, avoid darkness

avoid cars, avoid relationshits, avoid

poverty, avoid aggression, avoid advice

not to worry, meanwhile upstairs big

John lies still wounded by twenty years

of night shifts he couldn't avoid or quit.

II.

The Glock in my hand fits like a gangster's grip

slipped into my dreams, a pickpocketing he goes,

hear the New York soundtrack moving my sights

out of the motor and onto the dark hooded foe,

it's him or me, it's sin or sink, it's oblivion rushing

or the grey eyes of my sister crying a dry veined tear

boom is bang in slow motion, boom is bang in slow motion,

the film rewinds to before the first line and beyond birth

to the nothing that lives in the barrel of a cracked world.

III.

Not home for three nights the son has risen in someone else's eyes

she sets the cradle in motion but now he swings further and further away

she rubs the arms of the rocking chair until they are become her bones,

but he still burns in someone else's night, choosing the buck in the bang

over a mother's love, as she sits begging God never grants his death wish.

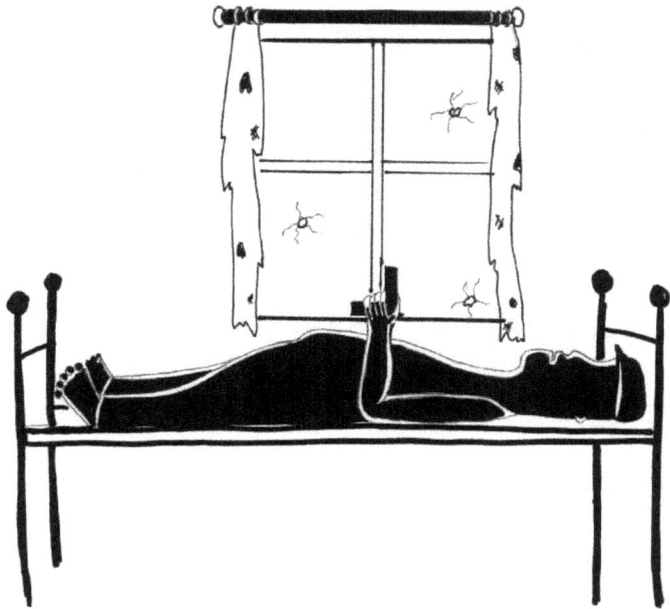

The Overcrowded Mind

too many fingers in your pie
too many strangers in your mind,
too many cooks to your broth
too many second hand opinions,
too many shame faced shamans
too many spies on your secrets,
too many tongues in your cheek
too many guests at your feast,
too many double agents
too many doppelgangers,
too many sugars in your tea
too many spoons stirring you,
too many waiters in your cafe
too many fingers in your till,
too many beans in the coffee
too many crumbs of comfort,
too many unbelievers
too many unfaithful,
too many demi-lovers
too many semi-sisters,
too many baby brothers
too many mother fuckers,
too many fingers in your pie
too many bearing you in mind,
too many non-special offers
too many basement bargains,
too many nosey neighbors
too many twitching curtains
too many keeping notes
too many stealing souls,
too many half cocked Buddhas
too many prying face booked eyes,
too many certain they are certain
too many truths told not be lies
too many fingers in your pie.

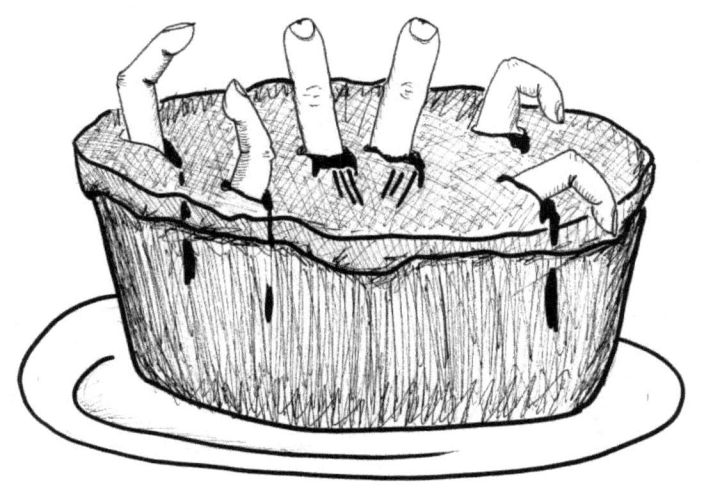

All work

'all work'

or pressure

will be brought

to bare,

'all work'

or minds

will be seized

by madness,

'all work'

or hearts

will be bullied

and burst,

'all work'

or find

your life

not worth

the living,

'all work'

or give

your kids

to care,

'all work'

or face

yourself

in their

spitting

image,

'all work'

until

old age

boxes

you

stupid.

All this worked

out by the boys

from Dallas and

Downing Street

on the back of a

bribe's envelope, see

the designs of many

glad hands chiseled.

"Arbeit macht frei" **

The gates begin

creaking again

a little a lot

then more,

bloody hell

re-opening

for business,

the roads paved

with badly sown

intentions.

'All work'

a burned deep

buyer's brand

smoking hot

like a coal

from Dachau.

Sing the song of all

When the biopsy comes back
I can't help but think
where the fuck is Spiderman
when you really need him?

Where is that Buddha boy
when loneliness strangles you
and the street poets sell out
for a hand full of applause?

When the Super Ego comes dancing
beside itself with sweet reflections,
where is the Woody Guthrie man
to sing the blues to our glories?

This machine kills fascists, the prophet's guitar made its promise. So,
where are the wire haired highwaymen when we most need them?
Where is the match to Blake's burning bow, to the ribbon of road?

O yes when the gold around your soapy necks
and the discrete metals in your mobile phones
come already blood stained from the Congo.

I can't help but think where the fuck is Tarzan
when you really need him, when black massacres
black to feed white greed for the earth's resources?

I can't help but think where the fuck is Buddha boy
when you really need him, when Olympic China
burns the world's ozone as it floats over old Tibet?

Yeah! Where the fuck is Spiderman
when you really, really need him?

This my diatribe

This is my diatribe making my space the only place of community
This is my diatribe making American war thought walk my streets
This is my diatribe making paper educated guesses into prejudices
This is my diatribe making Yankee gangster rappers poor people's masters
This is my diatribe making the drug of guns turn our children into toy soldiers
This is my diatribe taking Hollywood's unholy words as their new electro gospels
This is my diatribe making children without wings, making love without peace.
This is my diatribe against old powers making our new imprisonment invisible
This is my diatribe against the cash card manacles of money's all consuming madness
This is my diatribe against the doomed search for human power through violence.

This is my diatribe against the hopelessness of fear and shame and the thirty pieces of silver dollars jingling in my dead soldier boy's pockets and the I-pod god hanging from my red neck and the fascist wolf whistles raping my girl friend's angelic ear lobes and the evil preacher men preaching against men loving men or women loving women or everybody loving everybody and the rich bashing the ragged of the race and the squeezing of our bones for our marrow and the rich lips sucking out our sweet soul and replacing it with bloody warehouses of bloody things that no true human being ever needs and the white war against the black world going on and on without end.

This is my diatribe and I love them.

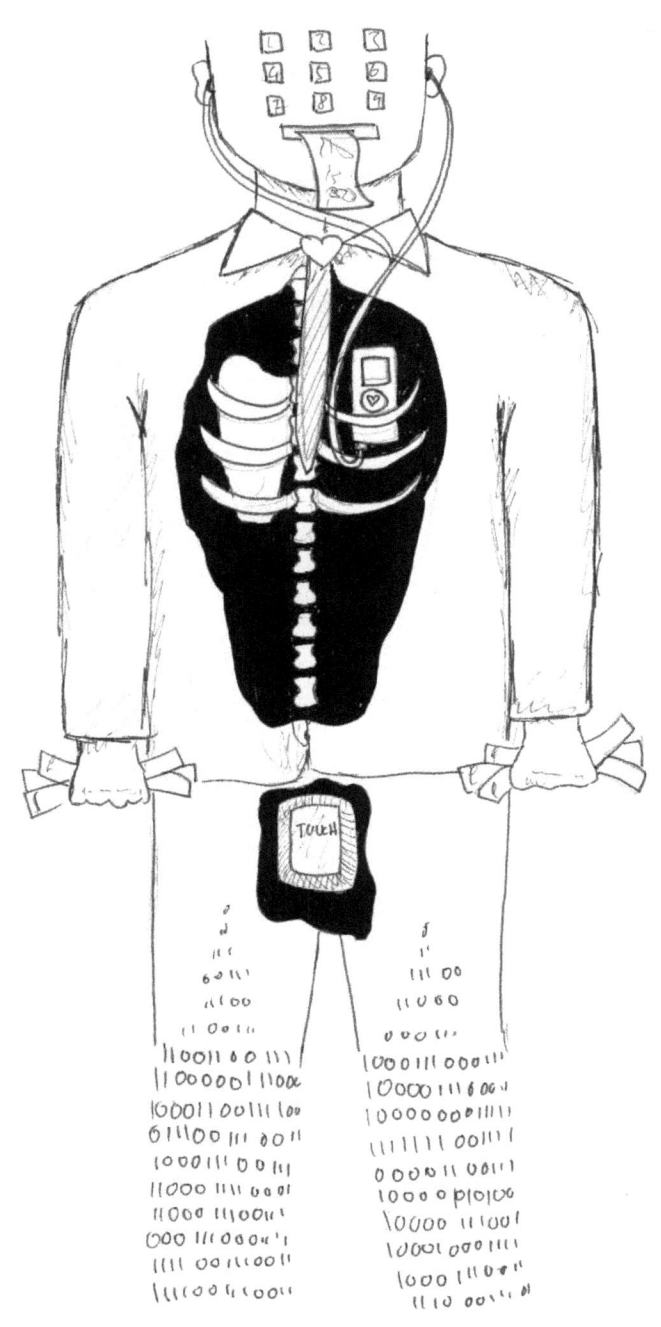

God's Working Class

A holy boy
sent to Priest
and brother us
on god's behalf,
sent at the age
of ten into black
forests of cloth
& burning wood.

A poor boy
sent to feast
upon the rich
man's vineyards,
his lips stained
red by Christ's
peasant blood.

An angry boy
sent to calm
down in the
garden of hearts.

Walking in pine
scented clearings
beside the lake
passing locks
through close
bitten fingers.

A boy far out
from home
tracked down
by gagging
unholy power.

Somewhere
over the years
he still lives
desperately,

trying to avoid

the unwanted
embarrassments
of men and their
hungry gods.

A lover's bargain plea

faraway and close faraway and close
the gentle trap in the singing kisses
of warm apple smiles dressed to thrill
faraway and close faraway and close,

dreams that money can buy dreams that money can buy
escape the mind's menagerie into love's wild sad interlude
and the daisy machines and the gadgets of our hearts
dreams that money can buy dreams that money can buy,

shake hands with the devil for god's sake
as he troops out of your shadow holding your light
turn off the moon piss on the sun pinch out the stars
shake hands with the devil for god's sake,

20 million years after we kissed the bone crumbled
our lips turned to coral our bodies to fucking fossil
we were never only human only angel only demon
20 million years after we kissed the bone crumbled,

how could you not bad trip on me
not feel the tinder wish on the burning pages
not gosh at the blues of my eyes on your skin
how could you not burn on my barricade,

mister you screamed for my whisper
thought you could smuggle me out,
could conjure love, counterfeit sin
mister you screamed for my whisper,

when the only thing needed was your love.

The Apolitical Poet

He had a slumber party in mind
And we were all invited.

His chosen method of suicide
Self-administered crucifixion,

He was brave before professors
Cowardly after the main events,

Wars, strikes, famines, murders,
Rapes, tortures, betrayals, poison,

Passed through him, human roughage
Passing through his wormy eaten soul.

He had a slumber party in mind
And we were all invited.

Dear reader can you refuse
Such a pleasant fire escape,

Such a feather bedded life boat
Of whimsical piss and vinegar,

Such a tip tap toeing around evil
Shushing us as if we were children?

He has a slumber party in mind
Are you feeling drowsy yet?

Or are you sitting
Uncomfortably?

If so then I'll begin....................

Revolutions ****

Copernicus seeded celestial motion
into every revolutionary movement

'De revolutionibus orbium coelestium'

Connolly arms tied by British murderers
played the atheist prey of good Christians

but knew the signs of coming eruptions
not a socialist Nostradamus a class Einstein

his sums work on the cell walls of prisons
each social equation tested on picket lines

the Parliaments of pubs, fields and streets
behind the equal signs sit prophetic answers

'Revolution is never practical until the hour
of revolution strikes — then it alone is practical'

as gravity spins a web of dead rocks and ice
black balls the matter of stars into planets

pulls the rabbit of life from dark interiors
so revolution brews and bubbles and digs

under the City God's unholy black jack economy
the mole of revolution is heading for the surface.

A fool's progress

Sometimes you make a ragged short-cut

a false conviction of an innocent victim

a final demand from one of the damned

sometimes you shake the tree too hard,

sometimes the windfalls of love bruise

loosen our tongues for wrong words

break open the crowns of our dreams

sometimes the stars burn like tears.

Sometimes love speaks with tongue in cheek

takes lightly the meaning of dark matters

sometimes the corpses of kisses haunt us

quiver the lips and chatter the teeth.

Sometimes you make a silent night scream

clip the dove's wings gag the lark's song

sometimes it seems life is in love with itself

a featherless god calling for suicidal flights.

Sometimes words are lost in amazement

or thrown down like a Roman soldier's dice

sometimes the shooting star guns you down

everybody wriggled with poisoned stardust,

sometimes you make a ragged short cut

a false conviction of an innocent victim

a final demand from one of the damned

sometimes you shake the tree too hard.

In the corner shop of apology

sweaty regrets hang from the ceiling

moldy salami souls drip spilled milk

broken oaths sit inside tacky toffee jars

occasionally rattle their Formica shelves

every time someone somewhere on earth

says "I love you" one hundred times and

only manages to lie once in a blue moon.

In the corner shop of apology,

the assistant would be covered in

unfinished tattoos, half whale, less heart,

more dagger, some mother, whole dragon,

and the names of girls he never knew.

In the corner shop of apology,

the air would be heavy weight with sorry

all conversations would be on one knee

soft chants of daily pleading would drift

through dog eared love letters never re-

turned to like me to you like you to me.

In the corner shop of apology,

I would exchange all my lucky charms

for the sweet everlasting gob stopper of your

sherbet covered finger snug on my tongue.

Love's Font ****

My mother does not recognize me

she only recognizes the kindness

that she put there in the first place

her love and care now loves and cares for her

she doesn't see me at all only the original loving

the first giving she gave returning to save her via

this unfamiliar man not being the beautiful boy

merely what she filled with love and now she dips

her fingers into me and blesses herself better

in the name of her father

and of her son

and of her holy ghost,

Amen.

The fragrant knife cuts the stinking rose

the fragrant knife cuts the stinking rose

the crush of the crowd does not last long

the rare edition gambled on the common

the comet's wandering finds the rogue earth

the rich paw at the beggar's heart until it gives up

the poor cast spells of revolution in between praying

the skull of mirrors makes everyone their own ghost ship

the syrup in your muscles sticks you to the suck up of serfdom

still the fleck of dreams in blue eyes pulls at your skin's uniform

still the ally wall puts my love on tip toe and shoots from the hip

hooray and the fragrance of life scents even the bullet's breath.

"O God! I could be bounded in a nutshell, and count myself a king of infinite space" —William Shakespeare, *Hamlet*

You could fly into your African mind's night tonight,

follow the day's shadow as it races across the ground.

A bird of dream swooping through the skull's armor

into the soft plumage of your sleeping wet cerebrum.

Plug into the images quivering under your covers,

Jump the gaps between atoms in the blink of a lie.

Bathe in the summers bubbling up from your raw chemical

springs before winter darkens in the dead ends of memories.

Massage each thought's bone for a moment's marrow,

scent a mother's cheap perfume as it stings your eyes.

Sense the convulsion of a lover's touch slowly hacking

into the cortex's mainframe, a nation of nerves enraged.

Night after night we are plunging into this thinking liquid,

searching for meaning inside the kingdom of the brain.

The Willy Wonker death camp

He was a porn flake, a cereal thriller,

a toasty darkness warm and spluttery on the tongue.

Yeah! That Jesus bread sure tasted like salt and leper

to this atheist's soul buds. Bring it on, godless god,

our thirst for life is the equal of your thirst for death.

He was a no man from the land of yes, under his breath

he fake danced and body sopped, avoiding the daily tongue

lashing of authority, the sun dead side of town his fiefdom,

the apathy bomb left him radiant inactive, scarred for life by truth,

where he now stays, a hidden amendment to the bill of shites.

He was a working talking sleeping stalking living dying voodoo doll,

worshipping the fascism of happiness, the fatal politics of party times,

dripping in passions of crime and the sob, sob, sob of so many sorrys,

he broke the heart's bank, flooded the mother lode, tried to father

a new earth, one where he could touch something that didn't hurt.

The answer my friend is not blowing off to see the wizard

not to follow the yellow brick road to the Willy Wonker death camp of dissident Umpa Lumpas,

maybe it's time to turn off obeying and tune in to the world's emergency call before you become

just another tin lion munching on a straw hearted world.

Revolution is a hard dream to sleep through, but some do

a deep dangerous seam to prospect, so they settle for the surface of things,

a secret boxing of one way blows, a deep down long time travelling hook,

an upper cut to the upper crust, you are the diamond mind

the money-bags man digs, he picks on you until you give,

until you are all played out, stripped, flooded and sealed off,

your body shafted, filled with the rubble of civilization, entombed

with all the other raped treasures, with all the other buried love.

Deference

Broken down and broken up
the mazy chains fall on us
mind binding in full practice
milked human kindness sour
deference drip fed in solution
one percent asked submission
make buy die birds being free
everyone knows not to dream
the island of Manhattan bought
with $28 dollars' worth of beads
your interval of time between
birth and death is being sold
a perfect teeth slim wasted
flesh object held as model A9
approved as long as it works
do not cry out the whip stings
do not dare release the pain
in some historical situations
it has been legal for owners
to kill their slaves slavery is rare
amongst hunter gatherer people
the high mountains are calling me
the wilderness inside seeks equality
to perhaps join a rebel guerilla army
and wait for the great red bat sign
to the fill the burning bloody sky.

You are here to go (the Rabbit Revolution)

We are frozen
not good enough
resignation accepted
deals with devils done
suffering death in life
ransoming every other
family for our own,

drinking love to sleep
feasting on sex to wake
sat at the back of the cave
guarding our precious bones
preferring the pitch of darkness
to the fall of shadows on the wall
cast up by the fire raging inside us,

a nest of rabbits caught in the middle
of the road, a mesmerized society
eyes wide as spinning dinner plates
waiting for dictatorship to swerve away,

but the driver has a death grip on the wheel
his bloody foot is nailed fast to the accelerator
he wants to feel the skin and guts in his tread
wants to wear you and feast on his road kill,

turn way from the light and choose your life
only action only your thump will save you now
to save your own skin know your own mind
and gather the colony, leave the nest and go!

You are here, to go! So go, go, go,
before you are eaten up by the road.

Run Obama, run

Society is suffering mental breakdown
its causes the same as JFK's in Dallas,
the replica bolt action rifle of poverty
is passed from hand to hand till it reach

Mr. Money bag man picnic king on the hempy knoll
he is much more than a patsy, he is the madness god
that fingers the trigger of each new holocaust's hit,
conspiracy complex? Yes it is, as serpentine as evil is.

Even with all the luck in the world order
life is one bullet you just will not dodge,
and you know the wealthy are the firing squad
proudly offering you a dollar rolled blind fold,

and a freshly depleted uranium tipped soul piecing round
sent seeking the heat from the beating hearts of Gaza kids.

Run Obama, you dumb trusting son of a gun!

The bankers have pulled the pin, handed you the grenade
retreated to a safe condo way out west, a day at the racists,
run Obama, they have locked you in the book depository
planted the next war, the great depression, the next atrocity,

I pray that you have no Jack Ruby brother, no native Judas
and that snow white has changed her color once and for all.

Daddy bought her a car

Her wildest Harley rides
wear gilt edged stabilizers

her each dangerous truth
comes already safely lied

even her lucky boots
are steely toe capped

even her luckless star signs
are diamonds in the smooth

funded by genetic cheque books
and bullet proof bank balances

her risky business dealings
soft landing on poor shmucks

her kisses taste of gum shield
and congealed bitten tongue

each smarty-pants bomb falls dumb
on her calloused ear plugged cochlea

even her lover's hot love
pools behind a dental dam

her heart of cold black pudding
jiffy bagged in a love proofed johnny

her radical t-shirt screaming 'Peace'
yes even her shouts are safe & soundless.

A Poet's Wish List

always drink from the edge of a crashing wave

burn holes in paper tigers with ember tongues

be a red angel flying on swept back blue wings

carry a dove spangled banner into the fiercest of battles

touch a stranger's pain at least once a day with your eyes

leave a trail in wet cement where your mind wandered

hide secret things, leave false clues, become unsolvable,

find undiscovered lands, burn the maps, wait to be found,

be found if you want to be, be lost if you wish.

Author's notes

* **Gunshawe**: Wythenshawe is a working class area of Manchester, England.

** **All work**: "Abeit macht frei" was the slogan hung above the gates of Dachau concentration camp. It reads in English "Works sets you free"

*** **Revolutions**: The word 'Revolution' as used to describe a radical change or over turning of the commonly held views was taken from Copernicus and his book *De revolutionibus orbium coelestium*.

Nicolaus Copernicus (19 February 1473 – 24 May 1543) was a Renaissance astronomer and the first person to formulate a comprehensive heliocentric cosmology which displaced the Earth from the center of the universe.

Copernicus' epochal book, *De revolutionibus orbium coelestium* [On the Revolutions of the Celestial Spheres], published just before his death in 1543, is often regarded as the starting point of modern astronomy and the defining epiphany that began the scientific revolution. His heliocentric model, with the Sun at the center of the universe, demonstrated that the observed motions of celestial objects can be explained without putting Earth at rest in the center of the universe. His work stimulated further scientific investigations, becoming a landmark in the history of science that is often referred to as the Copernican Revolution.

James Connolly (Irish: Séamas Ó Conghaile, 5 June 1868 – 12 May 1916) was an Irish republican and socialist leader. He was born in the Cowgate area of Edinburgh, Scotland, to Irish immigrant parents and spoke with a Scottish accent throughout his life. He left school for working life at the age of 11, but became one of the leading Marxist theorists of his day. He also took a role in Scottish and American politics. He was executed by a British firing squad because of his leadership role in the Easter Rising of 1916.

"Revolution is never practical — until the hour of revolution strikes. Then it alone is practical, and all the efforts of the conservatives and compromisers become the most visionary and futile of human imaginings. For that hour let us work, think and hope. For that hour let us pawn our present ease in hopes of a glorious redemption: For that hour let us prepare the hosts of labour with intelligence sufficient to laugh at the nostrums dubbed practical by our slave-lords - practical for the perpetuation of our slavery: For the supreme crisis of human history let us watch like sentinels with weapons ever at the ready."
—James Connolly

**** **Love's Font**: My mother suffers from Alzheimer's/Dementia.

Acknowledgments

We are grateful to these publications, in which some of this book's poems first appeared:

The Junkyard Procession — "The Apolitical Poet" / "Kill the Mickey Mouse that lives in your head" / "Revolutions" / "Deference" / "You are here to go"

Left Curve — "All Work"

Red Fez — "All Work" / "Gunshawe"

Speech Therapy Poetry Zine — "In the corner shop of apology"

A handful also appeared in John G. Hall's previous books *Bang!* and *Spleen*.

"The Overcrowded Mind" was first published as a Poems-for-All microchapbook.

Also from Crisis Chronicles Press

CC#64 — *Be Closer for My Burn* by Robin Wyatt Dunn
CC#63 — *#ThisISCLE: An Anthology of the 2014 Best Cleveland Poem Competition* by various authors
CC#62 — *I Don't* by Bree
CC#61 — *HOLDING STORIES in YOUR HANDS: Narrative Poems and Poetic Narratives* by Elise Geither
CC#60 — *The Night Market* by D.R. Wagner
CC#59 — *Ohio Triangle* by Alex Gildzen
CC#58 — *Poems for Explosion* by John G. Hall
CC#57 — *City of Tents: Poems About the Occupy Movement and Other Items Taken From the News* by Martin Willitts, Jr.
CC#56 — *Irises Made of Moth Wings* by Christian O'Keeffe
CC#55 — *Oct Tongue -1* by Mary Weems, John Swain, Steven Smith, Lady [Kathy Smith], Shelley Chernin, John Burroughs and Steve Brightman
CC#54 — *Songs in the Key of Cleveland: An Anthology of the 2013 Best Cleveland Poem Competition* by Various Authors
CC#53 — *Cut Me Free* by Ben Heins
CC#52 — *In Bold Blackness: Selections* by Jami Tillis
CC#51 — *Sunshine Liar* by Ryan Swofford
CC#50 — *YES, but....* by Martin Burke
CC#49 — *Every Bird, To You* by Sarah Marcus
CC#48 — *13 Ways Of Looking At Lou Reed* by Steve Brightman
CC#47 — *secret letters* by j/j hastain
CC#46 — *Cleveland: Point B in Ohio Triangle* by Alex Gildzen
CC#45 — *Rain and Gravestones* by John Swain
CC#44 — *Cheap and Easy Magazine, volume 1* by 36 authors/artists
CC#43 — *Bus Riders in the Storm* by Cee Williams
CC#42 — *My America* by Cee Williams
CC#41 — *The Everyday Parade / Alone With Turntable, Old Records* by Justin Hamm
CC#40 — *Howl for My Family in April* by Mary C. O'Malley
CC#39 — *Body Voices* by Kevin Reid
CC#38 — *the melody, I swear, its just around that way: volume 2* by Bree
CC#37 — *Grand Slam* by Alan S. Kleiman
CC#36 — *Red Hibiscus* by Heather Ann Schmidt
CC#35 — *Photograph* by Jackie Koch
CC#34 — *Queen of Dorksville* by Leah Mueller
CC#33 — *Angel* by Sandy Sue Benitez
CC#32 — *In Circles* by Ryn Cricket
CC#31 — *The Other Guy* by John Thomas Allen
CC#30 — *as she unbends* by Jolynne Hudnell
CC#29 — *Street maps for lost souls* by John Dorsey
CC#28 — *I Can Live with Death* by David B. McCoy
CC#27 — *The Wandering White* [broadside] by d.a. levy
CC#26 — *White Vases* by John Swain
CC#25 — *The Anarchist's Blac Book of Poetry* by Frankie Metro
CC#24 — *The Vigil* by Shelley Chernin
CC#23 — *This Is How She Fails* by Lisa J. Cihlar
CC#22 — *desire lines* by Chansonette Buck

CC#21 — *12 Poems* by Cee Williams
CC#20 — *Lens* by John Burroughs, a.k.a. Jesus Crisis [out of print]
CC#19 — *Primer for the Vanguard Youth* by RA Washington
CC#18 — *Only Human by Definition* by Jay Passer
CC#17 — *Rapid Eye Movement* by J.E. Stanley
CC#16 — *Grace, You Let the Screen Door Slam* by William Merricle
CC#15 — *the melody, I swear, its just around that way* by Bree
CC#14 — *Burnin' Shadows* by Kevin Eberhardt
CC#13 — *Fracture Mechanics/TRAP DOORS* by Michael Bernstein
CC#12 — *Unruly* by Steven B. Smith
CC#11 — *Blue Graffiti* by Dianne Borsenik
CC#10 — *Fever Dreams* by Yahia Lababidi
CC#9 — *Transient Angels* by Heather Ann Schmidt
CC#8 — *Identity Crisis* by Jesus Crisis
CC#7 — *Fuck Poetry* anthology by 40 authors [out of print]
CC#6 — *The Bat's Love Song: American Haiku* by Heather Ann Schmidt
CC#5 — *Suburban Monastery Death Poem* by d.a. levy
CC#4 — *Elyria: Point A in Ohio Triangle* by Alex Gildzen
CC#3 — *6/9 Improvisations in Dependence* by Jesus Crisis
CC#2 — *HardDrive/SoftWear* by Dianne Borsenik
CC#1 — *Bloggerel* by Jesus Crisis

And more titles coming soon by Susan A. Sheppard, Wendy Webb, Juliet Cook, Lyn Lifshin, George Wallace, Mark Sebastian Jordan, Eric Anderson, Margaret Bashaar, Kathleen Cerveny, Heather Ann Schmidt, David S. Pointer, Alinda Dickinson Wasner, Kevin Ridgeway, Austen Roye, Richard M. O'Donnell, William Merricle, Carolyn Srygley-Moore, Tracie Morell, Meg Harris, Steven B. Smith, Christopher Franke, Christopher Willard, Helen Shepard, Azriel Johnson, John Greiner, Esteban Colon, Jonathan Thorn, John Dorsey, Dianne Borsenik and Lisa Cihlar.

To get any Crisis Chronicles title, send ten US dollars to John Burroughs, 3344 W. 105th Street #4, Cleveland, Ohio 44111 USA. Or purchase via PayPal to jc@crisischronicles.com. Please add a few dollars for international orders.

www.ingramcontent.com/pod-product-compliance
Lightning Source LLC
Chambersburg PA
CBHW071242090426
42736CB00014B/3187